The Exodus Problem

My Journey of Deliverance From Anxiety, Depression and Chronic Pain

Isaac Nathaniel Gonzalez

ISBN 978-1-63961-534-6 (paperback)
ISBN 978-1-63961-535-3 (digital)

Christian Faith Publishing, Inc.
832 Park Avenue
Meadville, PA 16335
www.christianfaithpublishing.com

Special thanks to my dear friend, Jonathan Shepherd, for providing the cover art

Printed in the United States of America

This book is dedicated to my heavenly Father. Without His words of life, I never would have been able to make this journey.

I also would like to dedicate this book to my loving wife, Brandi, my parents, my family, and friends. Thank you all for being there for me through one of the darkest and most challenging parts of my life. Your love and encouragement will never be forgotten!

Introduction

If you are anything like me, and you have been fighting anxiety, depression, and chronic pain for any length of time, you may always find yourself searching for something to give you some hope. For me, I was always on the lookout for the next encouraging word that would give me hope to continue the fight. While I can't promise you that reading this book will help you overcome your current battles, I can tell you that you are not alone in your struggle and that there is hope. There is hope because there is a God that can overwhelm the thing that overwhelms you. There is a God who knows you, who loves you, and who wants you to defeat this enemy. If you have been searching for a sign or confirmation that you can make it, this is it! Think about it, God had you in mind when He inspired me to write this book, just to reach you. He loves you that much! He wants you to be free that much! So be encouraged because by the strength of Jesus Christ, you're not alone, and you can get through this.

The Shackle

Anxiety in a man's heart weighs it down.
—Proverbs 12:25 (NASB)

For as long as I can remember, I have always been a bit of a worrier. One of my earliest memories of worry and fear was being dropped off at school in kindergarten. For the first half of that year, I would cling to the leg of my mom/dad/grandpa, whoever had the difficult task of dropping me off at school. As they tried to drop me off, I would grab a hold of their leg and would hold on tighter than a lid to a pickle jar. I would scream and cry because I didn't want them to leave me and forget to pick me up. Looking back at those times now, I shake my head and laugh because whoever was dropping me off for the day really had to get creative about how to leave me at the school.

One of the best at dropping me off at school was my grandpa. Man, just talking about my grandpa really brings back some wonderful memories. I loved him so much, and I will never forget all the time he invested into me as a little boy. My grandpa went to be with the Lord in 2010, but I'll never forget how blessed I was to have a grandpa like him. I remember one time, we drove up to the school, and he walked me in and sat with me at my table in the cafeteria. I was eating my breakfast, and I felt so comfortable knowing that my grandpa was sitting next to me. I had a confidence about me that made me feel unafraid because I knew my grandpa was there with me. On this occasion, my grandpa used the classic "slip out when they are not looking" method. As I was wrapping up with my breakfast, the staff began their usual morning assembly and announcements for the day, and I completely forgot to check to see if my grandpa was still sitting with me. I look back on the moment now, and it brings some tears to my eyes to know that my grandpa loved me so much that he would sit there with me even though he probably had other things to do. As the assembly commenced, I remember being so caught up in what was going on that I completely forgot about checking to see if my grandpa was still there. Eventually I turned to check if he was still there, and to my surprise, he was gone. I don't know how long he had been gone, but I got to hand it to him because his timing was impeccable.

Looking back on those early years of my life, I can clearly see that I wasn't necessarily afraid of school or throwing a fit because I just didn't want to go to school. My fear was driven by a deep-rooted anxiety that I would be left at the school, and nobody would come to pick me up. When I think about this now, as a father of three, I see how irrational that worry was. But the thing about fear and worry is that it is never rational when you're actually going through it. The things that you fear and worry about can seem very real, especially the more you roll them over and over in your mind.

As I look through the different milestones in my life, I see that worry and fear were always close by and waiting to dictate my decisions. With each passing season, worry and fear took the form of anxious thoughts like "What if..." In elementary school, I would wonder what would happen if we had bad weather when I was at school. In middle school, I would often worry if my parents would be able to find the stadium that my team was playing at. In high school, I would worry about my grades. In college, I worried about graduating and paying the bills. And then finally, starting in about 2012, I began to worry obsessively about my health. At a glance, some of these worries may seem pretty minor or perhaps responsible worries, but the reality is that, little by little, I was becoming enslaved by my anxious thinking, to the point where these thoughts began to torment my mind. I didn't realize it at the time, but I was laying the foundation for one of the biggest mental strongholds that I have ever faced in my life.

Before going on to the next paragraph, take a moment to think about the biggest fear or worry you have in your life right now. What is it?

It was a typical Thursday for me on a warm September day in 2016. I was working full time at the church that I attended. I had been hitting the job hard, working late hours, and trying to setup a new administrative process. I needed a break and wanted to step away for a few days to just catch my breath. I had planned a long-weekend fishing getaway at the coast with my brothers and my dad. I hadn't been fishing in quite some time, and I was really looking forward to getting back out on the water. One of the fondest memories I have as a teenager is fishing on the boat with my family. Growing up, we never had a boat, and we would fish from the ledge or off a pier. Don't get me wrong. There is nothing wrong with fishing that way, but there is a whole other level of excitement and adrenaline that comes with fishing on a boat. I remember the excitement of backing the boat into the water, getting in the boat off the dock, listening to the soothing purr of the motor as the boat exits the marina, and then being filled with anticipation as the boat headed to the fishing hole. Such a wonderful mixture of emotions that I grew to really love and enjoy.

I was excited about the opportunity to finally go fishing again, except this time, there was something different about my anticipation toward this trip. For the first time, at the back of my mind, I had this fear that something terrible might happen to me on the drive to the coast. The typical route we take to the coast is filled with empty backroads and beautiful scenery, but also poor cell phone service. It was that last little fact about the trip that I allowed to be the catalyst for the anxiety that was beginning to well up inside me. *No cell phone service! What if something happened when we did not have cell phone service?* Being completely open and vulnerable, I was afraid of having a heart attack on a backroad while being out of cell phone service. I was afraid that if I had a heart attack, that would be the end of me. By the time my brothers could get me back in cell phone service range or to a hospital, it would be too late. I was afraid of dying on that trip. The irrational part of this fear was that I was a relatively healthy guy when I had these anxious thoughts. I was not dealing with any health problems and didn't have any health risks, so I really had no real reason to worry about having some type of medical emergency. It just didn't make sense to worry about it, but anxious thoughts are not rational thoughts.

The time came for me to go on the trip, and I said goodbye to my wife and kids and drove to meet up with my brothers. On the way to my brother's house, I felt a heaviness deep inside me that just made me feel off. I figured it was just nerves from the trip, or maybe even from the slice of pizza I had just eaten when I walked out the door. I brushed it aside and just figured it would eventually pass once I started to have a good time with my brothers. When I got to my brother's house, we loaded up in his truck and started to make our way to the coast. I still was feeling that heavy feeling like something was wrong, but I attempted to forget about it by talking with my brothers and just trying to have a good time. As we made our way to the halfway point, the point where cell phone services can get really sketchy, I felt an even heavier sensation in my chest and stomach. I remember trying to make myself burp so I could feel better. I would try to reposition myself in my seat to bring me some relief. Nothing was working. In fact, it was only getting worse. It got more and more difficult to participate in the conversation, and the anxious thoughts inside my head began to grow louder and louder and louder. The wheels of fear started turning, and the anxious thoughts started to flood out of me. *Is my stomach upset? Do I need to burp? Why is everything I'm trying not making me feel better? Is the discomfort I'm feeling a chest pain, or is it gas? Oh my gosh, am I having a heart attack?*

The fear came rushing in like a flood toward my internal dam that helped me keep it all together. I was using that dam to function at a high level despite being filled with anxiety. What I didn't know at the time is that my internal dam was cracked and was threatening to fail. The years of obsessive worry and anxiety had helped build that dam but was now causing damage to that dam. While everything looked fine on my outward appearance, just below the surface I was slowly but surely falling apart. This was the last straw. This anxious thought was the final worry that would break my internal dam to pieces. I was headed for a complete breakdown that would shake me to my very core and change the trajectory of my life forever.

As I was running through my head trying to analyze the situation, I noticed that my left arm was feeling tingly. That's when my worry went into hyperdrive. I no longer was part of the conversation in the truck, I was completely in my own head. Panic started to set in, and my heart began to race. My mind shifted to my worst fear. I started to worry that I was actually having a medical emergency in a place where there was little to no cell phone service. I frantically tried to find a way to alleviate the weird sensation in my arm and the heaviness in my chest. Then it happened. I felt an extreme spasm on the upper left side of my chest while simultaneously getting lightheaded and dizzy from the fear that I was dying. My heart was racing inside my chest, and I remember thinking that this was it. I had lost control of my ability to control my anxiety, and I felt like I was drowning and like the whole world was caving in on me. I had to get out of the seat, and I needed to get out of it right then and there. I frantically asked my brother to pull over, and I jumped out of the truck and began pacing up and down the road. I was in shock and scared and was so afraid of what might come next. I couldn't get my heart to stop racing, and I couldn't calm down. I distinctly remember in that moment that I had this irrational feeling inside me that told me that I needed to run as fast as I could run to get away and get to a safe place; but nowhere felt safe. Nothing felt like it could save me from my situation. I felt the foundation that I build my life on start to crumble. I was praying with everything in me, but the anxiety that I had allowed to grow and live in me all those years overwhelmed me. The anxious thoughts in my mind were speaking way louder than my ability to believe or even hear from God. Everything felt so hopeless, and it felt like it would never end.

After about fifteen to twenty minutes of me pacing up and down the side of the road and my brothers praying for me, I worked up the courage to get back in the truck and make my way back home. I remember being so afraid on the way back home. I couldn't trust my body anymore. In my mind, it failed me for no reason, out of the blue, and without warning. I was filled with anxiety, and I kept thinking to myself, *What if I have another attack?* I did eventually make it home and went to bed that night feeling okay, but the next morning when I woke up, I was met with the hard dose of reality that something had happened to me yesterday that I couldn't explain or even understand. I didn't know how to process this, much less live with the knowledge that this had happened to me. It left the door wide open for the anxious thoughts to take over. I was afraid of this happening again, and I was afraid that it could happen at any time.

Later that morning, my anxious thoughts eventually led to another attack, and I decided that it was time to go to the hospital to get checked. After all the tests were run, I was given a clean bill of health, and the doctor told me that I had suffered an anxiety attack. Even though the news was good, something in me didn't believe them. I thought something was physically wrong with me and that they had just missed it and didn't understand. Again, anxious thinking is not rational thinking, and anxious thinking ruled all my thoughts. I was broken in my mind and spirit. It seemed like in one day, I had changed from a functional guy to a complete nervous wreck. I was afraid to be alone, I was afraid to leave the house, and I was deathly afraid of having another attack. I didn't understand why these attacks were happening and therefore, in my mind, they could happen at any time and any place. Everything in my life was overshadowed by anxiety and fear of another attack. I became a shell of myself, and I lost myself to debilitating anxiety, depression, and chronic pain. The next two years of my life were complete hell on earth. I lost about fifty pounds and had retreated to a lifestyle that was absent of life. I stopped talking to my wife, my family, and my friends. I only communicated when I had no other choice but to communicate, and when I did communicate, I only talked about how terrible and unfair my life had become. The sole purpose of my life became about hoping to survive the day. My faith in God was shaken, and I was overwhelmed with the thought that life was over for me. I had nothing left. I was now a slave to anxiety.

Before we move on to the next part of my journey, I want to take a moment to give you some encouragement. I want you to know that your struggle matters to God and you matter to Him too. If you find yourself in a place today like I was in this chapter, I want you to know that it's okay and that there is hope. Stay with me and keep on reading because you can make it through this. Will you allow me to pray for our journey that we are about to go on together?

> Dear heavenly Father, I thank You for this wonderful person reading the pages of this book. Lord, I don't know what they are currently struggling with, but I know that You know all things. Lord, right now I ask that You step into their situation and lift them up. Give them peace, hope, and allow them to experience Your love, O Lord. Father, I invite You to go on this journey with us, and I thank You for Your grace, mercy, and love. You are worthy to be praised. In Jesus's name, amen.

When Enough Is Enough

Now it came about in the course of those many days that the king of Egypt died. And the sons of Israel sighed because of the bondage, and they cried out; and their cry for help because of their bondage rose up to God. So God heard their groaning; and God remembered His covenant with Abraham, Isaac, and Jacob. God saw the sons of Israel, and God took notice of them.

—Exodus 2:23–25 (NASB)

All my life I had been in church. My grandpa was a senior pastor, and both my parents are believers. My parents raised me and my brothers in church, so I knew the stories of God's awesome power and His love for us. I personally believe that up to this point, I knew of God, but I didn't really know Him. When I had my first major anxiety attack on that trip to the coast, I thought I was going to die. It was the first time in my life that I had considered my mortality. Those moments of sheer terror exposed a sobering reality in my life that I never knew I had. The reality was that God wasn't God in my life. He was the God of my grandparents and parents, but He truly wasn't God in my life. When terror struck like a thief in the night, I didn't have a real relationship with God to stand on. Embarrassingly enough, in that moment, I doubted everything that I thought I knew about God and my life. I was so afraid to die because I was so unsure if the things I grew up believing in were true. Being completely honest and vulnerable, some of the questions that ran through my head were questions I never thought I would have in my life. *Is God real? What if I am believing in the wrong thing? What if I only think I am saved, but it turns out that I have been believing in the wrong things?*

The fact of the matter is that I didn't know God in the same way those in my family who came before me did, and it was that hole in my life that helped usher in one of the worst times in my entire life.

The Bible tells us that "the fear of the Lord is the beginning of wisdom, and the knowledge of the Holy One is understanding" (Proverbs 9:10, NASB, 1995). Today, I have a deeper appreciation for this verse because I know for a fact that when God was missing in my life, nothing seemed to have a point. I lacked wisdom and understanding, that firm foundation I could find comfort in, because I didn't have a true active relationship with God. With my faith shaken, I fell into debilitating anxiety, depression, and daily chronic pain. I lost all passion for life and began to question the point of my life. I was lost, I was defeated, and I had no more fight in me. Day by day, I slowly lost the ground that made me who I was. My zest for life, my humor, my kindness, my courage, and my confidence and even my physical appearance all withered away slowly. My sole purpose in life was just surviving the day. The peak of my day was going to sleep at night so that I could escape from all the anxious thoughts that were tormenting my mind and my body. Rather than finding comfort in God, I began to slowly become dependent on the comfort of the shackle of anxiety to make it through my day.

I know it may sound weird to say that I found comfort in shackles, specifically shackles of anxiety, but take a moment to think about what may have shackled you right now? What in your life scares you or triggers anxiety? Is it easy for you to engage in activities that push that boundary, or does the thought of that terrify you? Imagine that you are terrified of heights, and you do everything in your power to avoid them if possible. Now let's say that someone close to you really wants you to go to a restaurant that's on top of a skyscraper. The table you are going to be sitting at for dinner is going to be a city view table that is set on a balcony that overlooks the city. It's a breathtaking sight for those who don't mind heights, but a real knee wobbler for those who are not a fan of heights. What do you do? Do you go? If you were afraid of heights, chances are just the thought of being that high and so close to the edge would be enough to make you feel anxious. Would it be worth putting yourself through the agony of all the anxious emotions just for dinner and time with a friend? Is it worth the physical discomfort, the self-loathing for feeling like a terrible friend because you ruined the evening with your anxiety? Is it worth feeling like a terrible friend because you spent the whole evening trying to hold it together and only gave your friend half of your attention?

For me, this type of thinking was a reality. The thought of going out and living my life was so burdensome and filled with worry that I began to be terrified to just leave my home. In my mind, I thought if I stayed home, I wouldn't have to go through those discomforts or pains. I would be able to have a "relaxing" evening and be in "peace." I put relaxing and peace in quotation marks because it wasn't really relaxation or peace that I was experiencing. I was slowly being subdued to the shackle of anxious thinking, all under the guise of safety and peace.

For me, the comfort of the shackle was found in being at home. Home was one of the very few places that I felt some sort of peace, and boy was I ever desperate for peace. At that point in my life, I would have done just about anything to get a moment of freedom from the vicious cycles of anxiety followed by deep depression. When I wasn't worrying, I was in a depressive state because of my overwhelming anxieties. I would only find relief from my depression when worry began to take back over. It was miserable, to say the least, and I was dealing with all of these while also fighting the most excruciating chronic pain I have ever felt in my life.

I had dealt with different kinds of pains all my life. I grew up as an athlete and had suffered various injuries, so naturally, I thought I was mentally tough; that is until I experienced the chronic pain that came with this battle. The pain I was dealing with in my back, neck, ribs, and chest was so bad that it often made it hard for me to think, to speak, and even to breathe. The pain was so constant and so stressful that it felt like someone was trying to tear my muscles apart. The pain would at times be so overwhelming that I would become nauseous, and the only thing I could do was just lay down to try to seek some relief.

I found myself constantly wanting to stay home to avoid putting any stress or unwanted excitement in life. I was doing everything that I could to be safe and avoid another terrifying anxiety attack, while also trying to avoid anything that would set off the chronic pain. This made the end of the day my favorite because I could lay down and escape my worries with sleep. I chose the comfort of the shackle because it made me feel safe. I did not have to let anyone down because of my anxiety, and I didn't have to deal with racing heartbeat, the sweaty palms and feet, or the overwhelming sense of the world closing in on me.

I had found a way to cope with my circumstances by waving the white flag of surrender. I wasn't going to try to fight to overcome the anxiety, the depression, or the pain. I was going to just live my life within the narrow boundaries that these tormentors allowed me to live in. This was just how my life was going to be from now on. Looking back on it now, I see just how much of my life I missed in those two years because I willingly chose the shackle over seeking after God.

For me, fear drove me to the comfort of the shackle, but what I didn't realize was that the comfort the shackle promised wasn't really comfort at all. The comfort of the shackle will encourage you to stop living life like you want to because it scares you into believing that anything outside of the shackle will be too much for you to handle. The shackle tells you to stay home because you will be safe, but the shackle is only doing what a shackle does best. It is allowing you to live your life on its terms. You can only live your life to the end of its chain. Rather than being free as God intended for us, we become slaves to the things that we fear most.

Unknowingly, I had stepped into my personal Egypt and had become a slave to the anxiety, depression, and physical pains I was dealing with. When this trial first began, I attempted to fight the good fight of faith, but eventually the weight of the shackles became too much. I slowly began to forget about the power of God and fell into despair. Safety, survival, and being free of pain became my new masters. The only thing I cared about was avoiding death. Nothing else mattered. I just wanted to be safe and feel at peace. It wasn't until my life started to crumble all around me that I woke up to the reality that I was losing everything. I was losing my family, and I was losing every good thing in my life. I realized that I was in trouble, and I realized that I needed to seriously examine my relationship with God.

I would like to tell you that I began to read the Bible, I rediscovered God, and He delivered me from all my troubles; but that's not the case. Most of my rediscovery of God involved me blaming God for my problems, for His lack of response, for allowing me to suffer as I was suffering. I would shout at God, cry out to God, and express my anger and frustration toward Him. I had believed in Him and tried to live my life right while growing up. I served at church, worked at church, and tried to help guide others in their walk with God. How on earth could God have allowed this to happen to me? What did I do to deserve such agony and torment? Why does everyone else around me have such a seemingly carefree, anxious-free, depression-free and pain-free life? Why was I the only one who was suffering? It just wasn't fair, and it seemed so cruel.

Eventually my accusations and questions turned into being vulnerable with God. For the first time in my life, I was actually being up-front with the Lord about what I was feeling. He began to show me that I didn't need to pray all the right words or hold my fears back from Him in order to stand in faith. He showed me that He wanted me to come to Him with everything because He wanted to help with everything.

> Be anxious for nothing, but in everything, by prayer and supplication, with thanksgiving, let your requests be made known to God. And the peace of God, which surpasses all comprehension, will guard your hearts and your minds in Christ Jesus. (Philippians 4:6–7, NASB)

All my life I grew up with the misunderstanding that I had to pray these perfect prayers to God in order to get my prayer answered. Maybe I am the only one, but my prayers were very calculated, and I planned to say all the right things in the hopes that my prayer would be answered. If I was dealing with a common cold or virus, I felt like I had to approach God in faith. Instead of saying a prayer that is open and vulnerable like this: "God, please help me because I feel terrible, and I can't take feeling like this anymore. I believe that by the stripes of Jesus Christ, I am healed, so I ask in the name of Jesus for healing and deliverance from this. Amen," I would pray something like this: "God, thank You that I am not sick and that my body is healed. Thank You for Your healing power. In Jesus's name. Amen."

God exposed that my prayer life was lifeless because it lacked vulnerability. I wasn't inviting God into my situation; I was treating Him like a math formula to solve my issues in life. I would only come to Him when I needed something, and even when I did come to Him, there was no relationship involved in the interaction. It was this revelation that threw the floodgates of my heart open. I broke down and gave it all to Him. I told Him about the deepest darkest fears that I was afraid to think about. I told Him about the doubts I had in my relationship with Him. I told Him how I just couldn't see a way out of this anguish and how I was afraid I would never make it out.

> And the sons of Israel sighed because of the bondage, and they cried out; and their cry for help because of their bondage rose up to God. So God heard their groaning; and God remembered His covenant with Abraham, Isaac, and Jacob. God saw the sons of Israel, and God took notice of them. (Exodus 2:23–25, NASB)

I had finally cried out to God. I no longer wanted to try to just cope and exist in my mess. I no longer wanted to be in bondage. I was tired of living my every waking moment in fear. Enough was enough. I was finally ready to leave my Egypt.

Before we move on to the next chapter, I wanted to encourage you to be open with God about your struggle. God loves you where you are, and He is ready to listen and bring peace to your mind and heart. He loves you, and He is ready to help. If you feel like you've been holding back things from God, whether out of fear, shame, or even religion, take a step of faith and take this moment to be open and real with Him. You can do this! Will you please allow me to stand with you in prayer?

> Father God, I thank You for the person that is reading this book. Lord, though I may not know them by name, You do. You knew this reader before they were born, and You know the pain and struggle they are going through in life right now. Father, I ask You to help give them the courage and boldness to be open and real with You like they never have before. I ask, in the name of Jesus, that those walls will come down and strongholds will be broken. Bless this reader and allow Your peace that surpasses understanding to surround them. Oh, Lord, overwhelm the very thing that is trying to overwhelm them. I thank You, Lord, for Your loving-kindness and mercy. In Jesus's name, amen!

Deliverance Is a Journey

Moses said to the people, "Remember this day in which you
went out from Egypt, from the house of slavery; for by a
powerful hand the Lord brought you out from this place."
—Exodus 13:3 (NASB)

If you're anything like me, you might be tempted into thinking that one victory over a struggle means complete victory over the entire situation. As you probably already know, this is simply not true. A victorious battle doesn't guarantee the end of your struggles. One of the most important lessons that I learned through this experience is that deliverance is a journey. Deliverance is not automatic, and it doesn't come easily. I was asking God to deliver me from a major stronghold in my life, and I also had it all worked out in my head just how God was going to deliver me. Images of Jesus healing the lame, causing the blind to see, and raising people from the dead filled my mind, and I began to see myself just waking up one day and everything is gone. The tormenting anxious thoughts, the dark clouds of depression I would feel on and off every day, and the debilitating pain, everything…just gone! As convenient as that would have been, it just didn't work out that way for me. My desire to be delivered required me to take steps of faith that were beyond my comfort zone. It required me to push myself harder and to go further than I was capable of going. It was a journey that was impossible for me to complete on my own strength, but it wasn't impossible for God.

When the disciples heard this, they were very
astonished and said, "Then who can be saved?"

> And looking at them, Jesus said to them, "With people, this is impossible, but with God, all things are possible." (Matthew 19:25–26, NASB)

I can't imagine anyone could identify with the struggle of taking on an impossible task more than the Israelites leaving Egypt. After 430 years in bondage (see Exodus 12:40), Pharaoh finally let the people of Israel go because God showed up in so many big ways for Israel. Pharaoh had repeatedly refused to let the people of Israel leave Egypt, and each time he refused, God sent a plague to the land. Each time a plague came, Pharaoh would cry out to Moses to entreat the Lord to stop the plagues. When Moses would cry out to the Lord, God would remove the plague, and Pharaoh's heart would grow hard, and he would again refuse to let the people of Israel leave Egypt. Pharaoh had seen God turn a rod into a serpent, water into blood. He saw how he sent frogs, then flies, that covered the land. He saw the Egyptian livestock struck down with pestilence and disease. He saw boils that covered the Egyptians and the animals. He saw the hail that caused great destruction. He saw locusts that ate the crops and a terrifying darkness that covered the land for three days. Yet after all these awesome displays of God's power, Pharaoh still refused to free Israel from bondage. It wasn't until after the final plague that cost Egypt and Pharaoh the lives of their first born that he finally relented and sent Israel out of Egypt.

Side note: I highly recommend checking out Exodus 7–12 for the full story with all the amazing details of how the Lord came through for His chosen people. It really is an awesome testament to just how much God loves His people and how much He wants us free.

After the final plague, Israel was set free from their bondage and, for the first time since the time of Jacob, they were able to experience freedom. And they would all live happily ever after, right? Nope, not even close! What they soon found out was that their deliverance wasn't automatic. Sure they had been physically freed from slavery, but they still needed deliverance in their hearts and minds. Deliverance was a journey that they had to take in order to receive the true freedom they wanted so badly. They were excited to be free, but they soon found that the journey they were on would test their desire for freedom and would expose where they truly placed their hope and faith.

Jumping back into my journey, I had a breakthrough in my prayer life with God, but my actions before this breakthrough had left my life in shambles. Every major area of my life was going through critical failure. My marriage, my relationships with my kids, my family, my friends, my job, and most importantly, my faith were all severely impacted by the shackles of my struggle. All the dearest parts of my life were withering away, and it felt like there was nothing that I could do to stop it. I felt like a runaway freight train heading straight for my own destruction. I felt my life spinning out of control, and it felt like there was nothing that I could do to stop it. I truly had this overwhelming feeling like the end, for me, was near and because of that I found it very hard to do anything except wait for the day of my death to come. As hard as I would try to be positive and try to envision a future, my mind just wouldn't allow me to go there. Depression had a vice grip on my ability to see a future and my ability to find joy in life. I remember I would just sit for hours at a time, just lost in my thoughts and sadness. I was lifeless and at the end of my rope. I was done. The only thing I could do at that point in time was just cry out to the Lord for help. Everything in me hoped that He would answer, and answer me He did!

One day I was at church and struggling as usual when I left my house. I was doing everything that I could to quiet my anxious thoughts and truly just focus on giving praise to God. Back then, it really was a battle and a task to focus because the anxiety, depression, and pain had a choreographed routine that, up to that point, would completely destroy me. Each battle would begin with me just feeling anxious in general. It was so bad that I was anxious that I was going to be anxious, anxious that the chronic pain might flare up, and anxious about the fact that I may be causing my own problems by being anxious. Then the pain would begin. My tension from being anxious would cause my chest muscles to spasm, my jaw to ache, my back to begin to spasm, and my ears to start ringing loudly. I say ringing, but it was more of a hissing; a hissing that was so loud that it was dizzying. Then the anxiety would ramp up even more, and scary thoughts like medical emergencies and death began to run through my mind like ants on an anthill that had just been smashed. Then after eventually calming down, the depression would anchor the whole process by sending me back to the dark dungeon of my own sadness. I was trapped by the weight of the reality that was my wretched life. I would be destroyed for days on end, unable to escape the long, jagged daggerlike grip of depression. The barrage of thoughts that something was wrong with me, that I was a hopeless case, that my life could never get better, and the thought that there was no hope for a future would overwhelm me. Then when the depression started to fade, the whole process would start all over again.

It was during one of these battles that the Lord spoke to my spirit. His voice broke through my tormenting thoughts almost as if someone had clicked the mute button on the worries in my heart. The roar of my worry was completely silenced by the still and small whisper of the Lord. Like God did for His chosen people, Israel, He showed up for me. I felt God telling me to go home and look at an old planter that we had sitting in our front flower bed, and He told me that what I was going to find in that planter was going to be symbolic of the work that He was about to do in my life.

You may be thinking to yourself, *What is the significance of a planter? Why would God choose that of all things?* To be honest, I had the very same questions and doubts. This planter, at one point, had a plant in it that we never watered or cared for. Eventually, after all the neglect, the plant died. The planter sat on our front porch with the dead plant, and as time passed, the soil dried out and became brittle. It was neglected and an eyesore, but for some reason, I couldn't bring myself to throw it out. Eventually, after a few months of it sitting on our porch dead, I moved the planter out of sight in our front flower bed. I got tired of seeing the dead plant at the front door, but I didn't just want to throw it away, so the front flower bed behind a bush seemed like a great place to put it out of sight. Weeks, if not months, went by, and the planter continued to sit uncared for and without water. It continued to be neglected and passed over, until God reminded me of it on that life-changing day at church.

After church, my family and I came home, and I remembered that the Lord had moved me to look at the plant in the flower bed. As I began to walk to the flower bed, I felt a mix of emotions running through my mind and body. I almost immediately became anxious and fearful. *What if I really didn't hear God? What if I did and what I was going to find in the pot would be an answer that I didn't want to hear?* I slowly walked to the flower bed and looked down into the planter and immediately burst into tears. I sobbed with an overwhelming feeling of being loved because in that forgotten planter was a brand-new seedling that had sprung out next to the dead plant. I was completely overwhelmed and at a loss for words. There was absolutely no way, in the natural, that any plant should be alive in that planter. The soil was so dry and brittle that the weeds didn't even dare to grow in the planter. Despite all this, there it was, so beautiful and green. It was perhaps the most beautiful thing I had ever seen. The seedling was so full of life and strong, and it gave me the encouragement that I needed to be able to move forward. It truly was a miracle and gift from God! He loved me, He knew me, He knew my struggle, and He was going to do a new work in me.

The Lord had spoken. Through this miracle, He revealed His plan for my life. In my mind I was the dead plant. I once was planted in good, nurturing soil but overtime, I had neglected my relationship with the God of my fathers and began to take on the world in my own strength. When the fear and anxiety that I had delt with all my life finally overwhelmed me, I was like that dead and dry planter. I no longer was planted in a consistently-watered and nutrient-rich environment. All my life and strength had withered away until I was dead inside. It resulted in my struggles becoming too much, and I felt the only thing left to do in my life was to die just like that plant, but God had other plans.

> The righteous cry, and the Lord hears and delivers them out of all their troubles. The Lord is near to the brokenhearted and saves those who are crushed in spirit. (Psalm 34:17–18, NASB)

Even though I had drifted so far away from God, He had never left me. He heard my prayer and spoke life into my situation. He had called life into a dead planter, and He was calling life back into me. He showed me that though the life I had known before the attack had passed away, He intended to create a new life in me that would deliver me from the shackles of anxiety, depression, and pain. He showed me that, like the seedling I found in the planter, He was going to use the conditions of my circumstance to propel me out of my slavery and into the true freedom that I would find in Him.

After seeing this miracle from God, I immediately felt empowered and full of confidence. I remember thinking to myself that the struggle was over. I felt that since God had spoken, it only made sense that He had delivered me from my agony. I could finally go back to living my life and not have to spend my every waking moment in fear. It felt as if the weight of the world was taken off me. It felt like I had woken up from a terrible dream and found to my relief that the nightmare was only a dream. I went to bed that night pumped, the nightmare was over, and I was ready to take on the next day. The next day came, and like clockwork, there was anxiety, depression, and pain waiting to greet me. I'm not going to lie; I was extremely disappointed because I had thought all this was behind me. As much as I wanted the Lord to miraculously heal me so I could continue about my life, I quickly learned that His promise of a new life was not going to be automatic.

At first, I was angry with God all over again for not healing me and not delivering me from my turmoil immediately. I remember questioning God's plan and even accusing Him of not caring and being cruel for allowing me to continue to suffer. Why show me the plant? Why promise me new life? My life didn't seem new to me; in fact, it felt like the same old story, just a different day. Like any step of faith, I had to make a choice on what I was going to do moving forward. Was I going to fall into self-pity and reject the word of the Lord because He didn't deliver me in the way I expected Him to, or was I going to trust Him and seek to find out what His plans were for my deliverance?

In life and as believers, I think we often find ourselves crying out to God for help and then becoming discouraged when He doesn't answer according to our plans. It's during these challenging times that the Lord likes to remind me of Naaman in 2 Kings 5. In case you are not familiar with the story, here is a summary of what happened to Naaman. By the way, whether you are familiar with this account in the Bible or not, I would highly recommend that you check it out because it's so powerful and relatable to the circumstances that you may find yourself dealing with.

Naaman was a captain in the army of the King of Aram. He was highly respected in his land, and because of his faithfulness to his master, the Lord had allowed him to be victorious in battle. Despite so many things going well for Naaman, he had leprosy, and there was no real hope for a cure until Naaman heard from an Israeli captive that there was a prophet in Samaria who could cure him of his leprosy. Naaman eventually tracked down Elisha after receiving permission from the King of Aram and had high hopes for a miracle. When Naaman arrived at the place where Elisha was staying, Elisha sent a messenger to Naaman and instructed him to dip himself in the Jordan River seven times, and he would be cured. I must admit that Naaman reacted in a way that I probably would have.

> But Naaman was furious and went away and said, "Behold, I thought, 'He will surely come out to me and stand and call on the name of the Lord his God, and wave his hand over the place and cure the leper.' Are not Abanah and Pharpar, the rivers of Damascus, better than all the waters of Israel? Could I not wash in them and be clean?" So, he turned and went away in a rage. (2 Kings 5:11–12, NASB)

Naaman was furious at the fact that things did not play out like he had thought they would. He didn't understand why Elisha wouldn't even bother to see him and why he was being told to go do something that really didn't make sense to him. In his frustration and confusion, he decided to leave, but eventually he was encouraged by one of his servants to heed the word of Elisha.

> Then his servants came near and spoke to him and said, "My father, had the prophet told you to do some great thing, would you not have done it? How much more then, when he says to you, 'Wash and be clean'?" So he went down and dipped himself seven times in the Jordan, according to the word of the man of God; and his flesh was restored like the flesh of a little child and he was clean. (2 Kings 5:13–14, NASB)

Thank God for the servant who was willing to encourage Naaman to obey the word of the Lord! Had Naaman chose to not obey the word of the Lord, I'd like to assume that he probably would have lived the rest of his life a leper and would never have experienced the healing power of God. When I read this account, it's easy for me to judge Naaman for not just listening to the word of the Lord spoken through the prophet Elisha. Why would he react so poorly and risk missing out on being cured? Why would anyone want to reject the plan God has because it wasn't exactly like they planned it out? Doesn't God know better?

Even when His plan doesn't seem to make sense or line up with our timing, His way is better. Circling back to where I left off in my story, I, like Naaman, was left with a choice. Would I stay angry and just give up because my deliverance didn't pan out like I had planned, or would I choose to trust God? As hard as it was to accept that my deliverance wasn't going to be automatic, I chose to trust God.

Before we move on, I truly feel it in my heart to encourage you in your situation right now. God loves you dearly, and He knows the struggle you are dealing with. He has a plan for you, and He will be with you every step of the way on your journey. Stand strong, trust the Lord, and resist the temptation to give up. The Apostle Peter tells us in 1 Peter 5:9 to "resist him, firm in your faith, knowing that the same experiences of suffering are being accomplished by your brethren who are in the world." Take heart in knowing that you are not alone in this and that there is an entire community of believers who have gone through similar struggles. There is hope, and you can get through this!

> Father God, I thank You for Naaman's servant who spoke up and encouraged Naaman to heed Your word. I thank You for the account of Naaman and the encouragement it gives us to trust in You, even when it doesn't make sense. Lord, thank You for reminding us that Your ways are higher and that You have good plans for us. Father God, I ask in the name of Jesus that You give the reader boldness, strength, endurance, and courage to trust Your way. Lord, I ask that You be with them and allow them to feel Your presence as they step out in faith. Lord, thank You for loving us dearly and never giving up on us. Thank You for Your willingness to rescue us from self-inflicted slavery and for the mercy You extend to us as we embark on the journey of deliverance. In Jesus's mighty name, amen!

Old Masters Die Hard

Then the Egyptians chased after them with all the horses and chariots of Pharaoh, his horsemen, and his army, and they overtook them camping by the sea, beside Pi-hahiroth, in front of Baal-zephon. As Pharaoh drew near, the sons of Israel looked, and behold, the Egyptians were marching after them, and they became very frightened; so the sons of Israel cried out to the Lord. Then they said to Moses, "Is it because there were no graves in Egypt that you have taken us away to die in the wilderness? Why have you dealt with us in this way, bringing us out of Egypt? Is this not the word that we spoke to you in Egypt, saying, 'Leave us alone that we may serve the Egyptians'? For it would have been better for us to serve the Egyptians than to die in the wilderness."
—Exodus 14:9–12 (NASB)

After God showed me the miraculous sign in the dead and forgotten planter, I had a burst of confidence and a slight glimmer of hope. I thought to myself that there just might be a possibility that I could get relief from my daily anguish. I knew that my deliverance was going to be a journey, but it was one that I was determined to make. I set my heart and confidence on the promise and miraculous sign that God had shown me. While there was some initial disappointment on not just being miraculously healed, I did take comfort in the fact that the Lord showed me that He was going to make my life new through this battle with anxiety, depression, and chronic pain. To this day, I am so thankful that God chose to speak to me through that planter in my front flower bed. It was the word that I needed to be able to break the shackles of anxiety, depression, and pain. There is just something about a word from God that can completely lift the weight of the world off your shoulders.

Rejuvenated and reencouraged by the story of Naaman, I began my journey unsure of what to expect. Was I still going to deal with overwhelming anxiety or crushing depression and pain? I wasn't sure, but I was ready to be done with this battle, so I pushed ahead in faith by trying to go back to living my life. As I embarked on my journey I would wake up with a renewed sense of adventure and hunger to enjoy life, but unfortunately, that courage and boldness seemed to melt away, like ice in direct sunlight, the moment I sat up from my bed. I would wake up from what seemed like the sleep of forgetfulness, and for that brief minute or two when I was waking up, I had that glimmer of my old self. In those brief moments, I didn't remember the attack I had, or that I was dealing with constant anxiety, depression, and pain. There was just a sense of joy to be awake and to start a new day. Unfortunately, those moments didn't last long before the flood of anxious thoughts, pains, and depression started to beat down the door to my spirit, mind, and body.

Before I was hit with overwhelming anxiety, depression, and pain, I was the type of person that was a go-getter, one that was always up to try something new, and a person who was always ready to prove doubters and naysayers wrong. When I was in elementary school, I remember someone a couple of grades older than me telling me that there was no way I could read the book *Old Yeller*. All that did was motivate me to check out the book, read it, and get a 100 percent mark on the reading test for that book. Deep inside me, I had this confidence that I could do anything that I set my mind to, despite what other people would say.

There was a time in high school when I needed to get to summer football practice, but I hadn't learned how to drive stick on a vehicle yet. So what did I do? I jumped in the truck and figured out how to drive myself to practice. It wasn't the smoothest ride, and I killed the engine a few times at the light, but I made it. Don't get me wrong; I was absolutely terrified the entire drive. I was especially nervous when I would stall out the vehicle at a busy light with people waiting behind me to get moving. Talk about pressure! It was frightening, and there was a lot of pressure, but there was a deep drive in me to overcome this impossible challenge.

In college, I was told that the relationship I had entered with the most wonderful woman in the world would never last, but by the grace of God, we have just recently celebrated our eleventh year of marriage. I was told that I didn't understand love and that we were both into each other for all the wrong reasons, but deep in my heart, I knew there was something very special about this woman. The naysayers couldn't sway me or cause me to doubt my feelings for her.

Finally, one other example of the type of person I was before the attack is that I learned to ride a motorcycle, passed the safety test and driving test in one weekend, and drove eighty-plus miles round trip to work the first day I got my motorcycle license. There was a deep desire in me to enjoy my life and not shy away from the things that traditionally scare most people. Sure there were lots of dangers and potential hazards that came with riding a motorcycle, but I wasn't going to let that stop me from enjoying a motorcycle.

I was born with a desire to succeed and not back down from a challenge. I have always had a deep desire in me to overcome and excel at what I put my hand to. While there were certainly things that came up in life that frightened me, I always took the challenge with confidence that I would be able to overcome it. I was comfortable in my own skin and had major confidence in my gifts and my abilities. It seemed as if the possibilities and opportunities for my life were endless, until they weren't.

In the account of Israel's exodus and deliverance from Pharaoh and Egypt, we see that shortly after being set free and told to leave Egypt, the Israelites find themselves trapped between the Red Sea and Pharaoh's charging army.

> Then the Egyptians chased after them with all the horses and chariots of Pharaoh, his horsemen and his army, and they overtook them camping by the sea, beside Pi-hahiroth, in front of Baal-zephon. (Exodus 14:9, NASB)

Even though Israel had been set free, their old master changed his mind and was determined to get them back. Pharaoh was determined to bring Israel back into bondage and back to the shackles of slavery. With the might of Pharaoh's chariots roaring upon them, and an impassible sea at their backs, all seemed lost. Deliverance seemed like a cruel dream that they were about to be awakened from. It seemed easier to just return rather than die. It seemed logical to return to the shackle and its false sense of security rather than perish.

> As Pharaoh drew near, the sons of Israel looked, and behold, the Egyptians were marching after them, and they became very frightened; so the sons of Israel cried out to the Lord. Then they said to Moses, "Is it because there were no graves in Egypt that you have taken us away to die in the wilderness? Why have you dealt with us in this way, bringing us out of Egypt? Is this not the word that we spoke to you in Egypt, saying, 'Leave us alone that we may serve the Egyptians'? For it would have been better for us to serve the Egyptians than to die in the wilderness." (Exodus 14:10–12, NASB)

In the past, when I would read this account, I would judge the people of Israel for being so fickle and quick to turn away from Moses and God. They only had been on the journey for such a short while, and they were ready to give it all up because Pharaoh changed his mind and was chasing after them. How could the people who witnessed the awesome power of God via the plagues so easily forget His promise to deliver them? How on earth could someone be so shallow and weak in the knees? It wasn't until I found myself being delivered from the shackle of anxiety, depression, and pain that I gained an appreciation for the situation that the people of Israel found themselves in that day.

The moment I would roll out of bed and my two feet would hit the floor, a flood of fear and anxiety about the tasks and events that

I had to do that day would begin to pursue me like Pharaoh and his army. Simple things like going out to eat, going on vacation, going to a party, going to the grocery store, talking on the phone to family, going to a meeting at work, and sometimes going to work suddenly struck fear and anxiety in me. I would dread the days when my family and I were scheduled to do anything out of the routine. All the small and simple things that once enhanced my life with hope and happy memories were replaced with irrational fear and worry. Things like upcoming vacations were no longer something to look forward to, but something to dread about. It was almost as if I had lost all confidence and courage to enjoy life.

I was trapped. I wanted to be delivered and to get on with my life, but the "Red Sea" of irrational fear of living my life again seemed to block my way. The roaring chariots behind me shouted out to me that there was no deliverance for me. I found myself doubting my deliverance, doubting if I really was being delivered. If God truly delivered me, why couldn't I do something as simple as going out to dinner with my wife without being terrified and full of anxiety? If I was truly delivered, why couldn't I talk to my own family on the phone without this dark cloud of anxiety and depression that would overshadow me and make me afraid to call them. It seemed to me as if my destiny was meant for the shackle and death. It seemed as if deliverance was wishful thinking, and I began to lose faith in God's promise to make my life new like that miraculous seedling in the planter. I found myself responding just like the people of Israel did. I had forgotten God's awesome power. I questioned His promises and questioned why He would tell me He would deliver me and leave me to continue struggling with the same old anxiety, depression, and pain. I was so quick to want to give up—again—and it just seemed easier to go back to suffering in slavery until my miserable life was over. Something in me had changed since the attack. Deep down inside me, the boldness and courage that I once had was now replaced with something new that would whisper doubts in my ear. It was a new voice that I had allowed to become the master over my life.

For me, the master I found myself fighting to be set free from was safety and security. I wanted to be safe in my health and in my life so much that I became shackled to anxiety, depression, and chronic pain. My "Red Sea" was the fear to live my life because, in my mind, it would compromise my health and safety. No matter how much I wanted to step forward and start living again, I would see that "Red Sea" in front of me, and I would feel the pressure of the chariots tempting me to return to the land of bondage. Something interesting that I learned quickly about this journey is that following God's plan will often require you to choose between succumbing to your fear or trusting in Him. On paper, this seems like an easy choice because God's ways are better, but this choice isn't as easy as it sounds because the "masters" that we allowed in our lives almost always will refuse to let go easily. My severe obsession with being safe and secure would not be so quick to let me go. I firmly believe that we often have "Red Seas" in our lives that test us to see if we will trust God, or if we will be scared and discouraged into doubt and completely miss out on the deliverance and perfect plan that God has for us. Jesus warns us of the danger of giving up and going back to slavery in Luke 11:24–26 (NASB):

> When the unclean spirit goes out of a man, it passes through waterless places seeking rest, and not finding any, it says, "I will return to my house from which I came." And when it comes, it finds it swept and put in order. Then it goes and takes along seven other spirits more evil than itself, and they go in and live there; and the last state of that man becomes worse than the first.

The truth of it is that going back would only make things even worse than they were before. I had to remember that the whole goal of the devil was "to steal and kill and destroy" (John 10:10, NASB), but Jesus came so that we "may have life and have it abundantly." (John 10:10, NASB) It's for this reason that God delivered Israel from the hand of Pharaoh by splitting the waters of the Red Sea and allowing them to cross through. (See Exodus 14:21–30.) God made a way where there seemed to be no way. He did it for them, He did it for me, and I know He can do it for you too!

For me, God parted the waters of my "Red Sea" by exposing the fact that I was terrified of having another attack. I was scared that my safety and security would be compromised if I chose to start to live my life again. He showed me that I was afraid I would come into a situation that would make me crumble, cause me to have an anxiety attack, or just be in a situation that would physically overwhelm me with pain from the anxiety. I can't tell you how many events, job opportunities, and fun I missed out on in my life because I was too afraid that I was going to have an attack while with other people. I was afraid that if others saw me struggling, they would ask if I was okay; and if they did that, then I would have a complete meltdown because then I would be terrified that maybe there was something wrong going on inside me, like a heart attack. It just seemed easier to not put myself in those types of situations.

God showed me that I was mistakenly thinking my deliverance was all on me and that my journey had to be done on my power alone. All my reasons for not doing something were based on me. I felt like it was up to me to hold it together when I started to spiral out of control with anxiety, depression, and my pain. I felt like I had to shoulder the whole burden. I hadn't realized that this journey would require more than what I could give. So I figured, if the battle was impossible, it's probably better for me not to fight the battle at all. It was just too draining and exhausting.

God showed me that at the root of all my fears, I was afraid that I wouldn't be able to stand up in my journey of deliverance and overcome the challenges and by-products of anxiety, depression, and chronic pain. I was afraid that I didn't have what it took to succeed or overcome the attacks. My first debilitating attack happened with my brothers on a trip. I couldn't hold it together then, so why on earth would I want to expose myself to more possible situations where I could potentially have another meltdown. I was afraid to fall apart in public and then have to deal with the suffocating depression that would come from the failure. It was just easier not to put myself out there than run the risk of not being enough to stand up to what terrified me.

These doubts wanted to keep me bound in slavery. Everything in me felt the weight and pressure of taking a step of faith because of my obsessive desire to avoid being in situations that could cause an anxiety attack. Once again, it seemed hopeless. It seemed like my old master of safety and security had me trapped with an impassible sea at my back. What was I going to do? I was trapped in my journey, and I couldn't see how I would be able to go a day without the tormenting onslaught of anxiety, depression, and fear choking out the joy of the day. I couldn't look forward to anything because everything I could potentially find joy in was overshadowed by the shackles of fear. Then when it seemed like all hope was lost, God parted the waters for me.

> But when they hand you over, do not worry about
> how or what you are to say; for it will be given to
> you in that hour what you are to say. For it is not
> you who speak, but it is the Spirit of your Father
> who speaks in you. (Matthew 10:19–20, NASB)

God showed me that I don't have to take on this journey on my own. I don't have to rely on my own ability to overcome my challenges or fears. I don't have to be afraid to live my life again because I could place my trust and confidence in the power of the Holy Spirit. If I started to feel an anxiety attack, deep depression, or pain taking hold of me in public, I knew that I could rely on the Holy Spirit to stand and speak for me. Wow! God wasn't calling me to step out and do it alone. He was calling me to step out in faith so He could fight the battles for me and help me truly be set free from my slavery. It was like the weight and pressure of stepping out in faith had been completely lifted off me because of this revelation. My deliverance was not contingent upon my ability to overcome anxiety, depression, and pain; it was contingent on my willingness to allow God to lead me in the journey. After God showed me this, I understood why going back to living was so hard and why things that should be joyful were filled with fear. I now had the confidence and boldness to step out in faith and begin to live my life again. Even though I was terrified to do it, I was ready to take on the things that I was scared to do because I had the confidence of the Holy Spirit to lean on. I had this overwhelming peace because I knew that even if things got stressful, painful, or overwhelming, I could rely on the Holy Spirit to minister to me and see me through.

When God split the sea for me, it was a life changing moment. God had made a way for me to cross over and escape the grasp of my former "master." With a restored faith and spirit, I began the next phase of my journey. Once again, I was ignorantly confident that the rest of the journey was going to be a cakewalk from here on because, with this new revelation that God showed me, deliverance was sure to be quick. Then came the desert...

Before we move on to the next chapter, I want to take a moment to encourage you in your journey. If you find yourself stuck between your "Red Sea" and the chariots of Pharaoh, I want to let you know that as much as you may want to give up, don't! I know it's hard, and you may not feel like you have the strength left to continue, but you can make it through this. Returning to the things that enslave you does not have to be your only choice. Cry out to the Lord! Be open and real; ask Him to show you His path to deliverance. Ask Him to show you where you may be holding back. God loves you, and He will never leave you or forsake you. Remember, He made a way for His people Israel, and He can make a way for you too!

> Dear heavenly Father, we come to You this day asking for Your mighty hand of deliverance, O Lord. We ask that You search our heart, know our anxieties, and show us the ways that are not pleasing in Your sight. Lord, save us from the temptation to return to the shackles of slavery. Save us from our own fears, insecurities, and doubts that we have in our lives. Give us the boldness and confidence to step out in faith into the journey of deliverance that You have set before us. We trust in You, O Lord, and thank You for Your grace and mercy. In Jesus's name, amen!

Grumbling in the Desert

When they came to Marah, they could not drink the waters of Marah, for they were bitter; therefore, it was named Marah. So the people grumbled at Moses, saying, "What shall we drink?"
—Exodus 15:23–24 (NASB)

I'll be completely honest—the next two parts of my journey were the most tiring, exhausting, and difficult seasons to get through. This part of my journey really put me to the test and challenged my faith in God's ability to deliver me to victory.

I, much like the people of Israel, had just experienced a major victory when the Lord exposed the fears that were holding me back and made a way for me to confront them in faith. My faith was at an all-time high, and I even had a bit of confidence and swagger as to how I viewed each day. I no longer had to dread going to a party or event because I had the boldness and confidence that the Holy Spirit would be there with me and guide me if I ran into any issues. I no longer felt weighed down by the pressure to be strong enough to stand on my own two feet in the face of adversity. I was confident that if I started to get anxious, the Holy Spirit would be there to rescue me from being leveled by an attack. I figured my game plan was foolproof and that it would be easily sailing from here on out. I was ready to inherit my "promised land" of rest and redemption from my struggles. I was ready to taste the sweet taste of victory of deliverance. After all, I've had two major breakthroughs. What else could God possibly have to show me?

Unfortunately, I quickly found that I had once again underestimated what this journey would require of me and just how much more God had for me to gain from the journey. I was like gums that hadn't been flossed in a while. The moment the floss pops between the teeth and starts cleaning, blood immediately presents itself. Just because flossing caused the gums to bleed doesn't mean it was bad for the mouth. In fact, the blood was a good indicator that the gums needed to be cleaned so they could heal properly. I learned through this step in my journey that there were parts of my life that had been neglected and needed healing. Each day the journey continued was painful, but like the floss to gums, each day I walked this journey I learned more, grew stronger in my faith, and I began to heal in areas that I needed desperate healing.

Around this time in my journey, I had accepted a new job. This was a big deal for me because the job I was leaving was only a three-minute ride from my home, while the job I was taking took about forty-five minutes to one hour to get there. Early in my struggle, just leaving the house for a three-minute trip to work was overwhelming for me. I couldn't make the three-minute trip without starting to panic and worrying that something was going to happen to me. All I could do was hope to make it back home at the end of the day. As I look back on this, I am shocked at how bound up I was by fear, and I am thankful that God loved me enough to not leave me in that state.

With a fresh vision of how to tackle my dread of doing anything outside of the routine, I took on the new job with courage and some degree of excitement. The job was a great opportunity to get back to doing what I loved. At work, my bread and butter are process improvement and data analysis. This job was going to give me a huge opportunity to start to put my hands on things that I enjoyed while also challenging my faith by taking me way out of my comfort zone. I had been struggling with anxiety, depression, and chronic pain for some time, and this was going to be my first time leaving the general area of my home. I was ready to begin a new chapter in my life. I was really hoping that taking this step of faith and going outside of my comfort zone would mean the end of my struggle with anxiety, depression, and pain. I couldn't help but think that maybe this was the act of faith that I needed to take in order to snap the hold that anxiety, depression, and pain had on me.

As I started my job, I had relatively decent days. I would go to work, do my job, go home, and feel accomplished for making it through the day; but honestly, it felt very lifeless. I was disappointed to find that even after taking the job and pushing myself to be bold and take on new challenges, I just didn't feel that sense of relief that I expected. Sure I was making progress and pushing myself a little more toward a life beyond the shackle of anxiety, depression, and pain, but they were all still present in my life. It felt like there was just a dark cloud constantly following me everywhere I went. I couldn't find joy in any aspect of my new job. I found myself subconsciously on edge and anxious while also dealing with a heavy depression. Nothing about this new season turned out the way I had hoped that it would, especially on the day that I had an anxiety attack at work.

That day started normally for me. I had gone to work and started chipping away at the project that I was working on at the time. The morning seemed to go quickly, and I was on track for another successful day until my cell phone buzzed. It was a text message from my little brother, Jorge. My little brother also worked at the same business I was working, and we would often see each other throughout the day in passing. We would try to eat lunch together when possible, and on this day, he texted me to ask if I wanted to grab lunch with him during lunch break. Unexplainably and automatically, anxiety started to well up inside me. Going out to get lunch was outside the normal routine, so I began to subconsciously tense up. But I was determined to allow the Holy Spirit to fight my battles, so I went with him to lunch.

We ordered our food and went and sat at a table. We started talking about work, but I couldn't concentrate on what he was saying. I was hearing the words he was saying, but my attention had become hyperaware of the anxious feelings that were starting to build up inside me. I tried to engage in the conversation and shook off the feeling by just trying to enjoy myself, but it persisted and continued to grow. As the discomfort only continued to grow, I started to feel overwhelmed and scared. I prayed under my breath for the anxious feelings and discomfort to stop, but I was met with silence. I began to feel the world starting to cave in on me again. The doubts that lived within me started to come alive, and my mind went into hypergear with all the what-ifs. As my mind began to race, it began to get difficult to breathe, and I felt my muscles in my chest and back starting to tense up. My heart started to race, and I started to get dizzy. I suddenly found myself in the frighteningly familiar place of a full-blown anxiety attack. I told my brother we needed to go back to the office so I could go home. My brother tried to ask me if I was okay, but I had no desire to speak or explain what was happening. I was drowning in the thoughts of panic and fear, and I crumbled. It felt like all the strength, boldness, and ground I had gained was completely lost. I felt like I was a seedling that had just taken root but had suddenly been ripped from the soil and thrown on the ground to wither away and die.

When I got back to my car and started to make my way home, I will admit, my first reaction wasn't to turn to God and the Holy Spirit to help me confront the anxiety and fears that I was facing in that situation. I immediately reacted in fear and started to think of all the worst things that could happen to me. *Was I having a heart attack? Was I having a stroke? What if the doctors missed something? What if this was it for me? Was I about to die?* As I started to think negatively, I found it more and more difficult to breathe. I got that overwhelming sensation to run to safety, but nothing felt safe. I felt so uncomfortable in my own skin. Everything in me just wanted to scream and cry because there was so much pent-up anxiety, fear, depression, and pain all coursing through me that it was just bursting out of me. It wasn't until I was in total panic mode and couldn't take the overwhelming feelings of anxiety that I realized that I hadn't even cried out to God or the Holy Spirit for help.

When I turned to God and cried out to Him, I expected immediate victory. I expected the Holy Spirit to tell me what I needed to hear to calm down, and I expected my pain to go away. Instead, what I discovered was a deafening silence. I couldn't feel God. I didn't get comfort by crying out to Him, and the anxiety and pain only seemed to continue to grow. I was crushed and completely deflated.

I remember screaming to God in my car, "WHY, WHY IS THIS HAP-PENING? WHY AREN'T YOU ANSWERING ME AND DELIVERING ME LIKE YOU SAID YOU WOULD?" I remember feeling so frustrated with God because I believed that He could deliver me from an overwhelming situation, but He wasn't saving me. I couldn't help but question how God could claim to love me, but allowed me to be overwhelmed and tormented. I asked myself, *What is the point of going through this? Why am I fighting so hard to be delivered only to seemingly fall just as easy as I did when I first started on this journey?* That familiar feeling of help-lessness and torment was starting to creep back into my spirit. I'm embarrassed to admit that even after receiving that miraculous sign in the planter and receiving His constant encouragement and love, I began to question God again. I began to question whether I truly heard from Him, and I also began to question if maybe there was no way back to a life without this torment. Something had to give because I couldn't keep doing this over and over in my life. I was just done. I started to grumble against God, and I was very tempted to just give up because it just felt too hard. I ended up going home, and I went straight to bed. I was just done for the day and didn't know what else to do or think.

When I look back on this season of my journey, I realize that I was probably experiencing similar emotions that the people of Israel were experiencing when they started to grumble against God and Moses shortly after crossing the Red Sea. After the people of Israel crossed the Red Sea, they began to journey through the wilderness, but had trouble locating water. With no water and very little hope of finding any water soon, the people began to grumble against God and Moses for allowing this dilemma to happen.

Despite the miracles, I still struggled to believe that God had the best for me, and I couldn't understand how the battles, especially the ones I was losing, were part of His good plan. Looking at the Exodus account in hindsight, it's easy to once again judge the peo-ple of Israel for being fickle and faithless to a God who consistently showed up for them. It's easy for me to wonder how a people could so easily forget just how powerful God really is and for me to arrogantly believe that the situation would be much different if I were in their shoes. The truth of the matter is that I was faring no better than they did.

I realized that I was struggling and grumbling in my own personal desert. I had expected the rest of the journey to be a cakewalk, but it wasn't. I had expected to quickly end the war with anxiety, depression, and pain, but that wasn't the reality of the situation. The moment it got hard, I began to question and blame God. It felt as if I was all alone and that God had forsaken me. I just couldn't understand why I was struggling so badly and why it seemed like God had little to say about the situation.

What I didn't realize at the time was that I was asking all the wrong questions. Instead of getting angry and asking God why He wasn't coming through, I should have been asking Him to teach me and show me what I needed to gain from the situation. The Bible tells us that "he who is slow to anger has great understanding" (Proverbs 14:29, NASB). I needed to do my best to quiet my anger and truly seek what God was trying to show me through the situation. During this difficult time, God reminded me of these verses:

> Consider it all joy, my brethren, when you encounter various trials, knowing that the testing of your faith produces endurance. And let endurance have its perfect result, so that you may be perfect and complete, lacking in nothing. (James 1:2–4, NASB)

> "For I know the plans that I have for you," declares the Lord. "Plans for welfare and not for calamity, to give you a future and a hope. Then you will call upon Me and come and pray to Me, and I will listen to you. You will seek Me and find Me when you search for Me with all your heart." (Jeremiah 29:11–13, NASB)

> Search me, O God, and know my heart; Try me and know my anxious thoughts; And see if there

be any hurtful way in me, and lead me in the
everlasting way. (Psalm 139:23–24, NASB)

When I stopped being angry about things not working out like
I hoped, I began to understand that God, in His mercy and love, was
using these hard and overwhelming circumstances to help me grow
and break free from something that was still stealing from my life.
Much like how a butterfly must struggle to break out of a cocoon
to gain the strength to fly, I had to walk through these struggles to
have the strength to uproot misplaced faith. I had anxious thoughts
that were stealing away my life, and the Lord wanted me to walk in
His everlasting way, but the only way to get to that place required
walking through this season. I firmly believe that if God would have
rescued me miraculously from the situation, I eventually would have
found myself back in the same situation at some point in the future.
God showed me through this experience that He isn't interested in
giving a temporary fix; He is only interested in bringing complete
healing that frees us from the things that hold us captive, even if it
means that we have to go through some challenges.

By allowing me to go through this struggle and many more like
it, God was able to show me that the anchor of my joy and peace
were still being placed in safety and security. I still had this deep-
seeded belief that I would find joy and peace again when I could see
that my future was secure. My joy and peace were contingent upon
a future that had me healthy, carefree, safe, and secure. God showed
me that attempting to find peace and joy in a secure, earthly future
was like chasing a mirage. I was chasing after something that I could
never reach. Even when it seemed like I was approaching that secure
future (getting back on my feet, taking on challenging things that I
had been shying away from, exercising to get healthier), the mirage
would quickly vanish and move further away. The moment one of
these items failed me, such as missing exercises or dealing with the
chronic pain, that mirage of security would fade away, and I would
get depressed and feel myself scrambling after that mirage to regain
my joy and happiness. It was a losing battle and a slippery slope that
I was trying to climb. The truth is that I was chasing something that

I thought I lost, but truly never had. A completely safe and secure life in this world is just not possible. There is always a possibility that something bad could happen regardless of where I am or what I am doing. The thought of this was unnerving to me, but it quickly exposed the fact that my joy and peace were anchored in something that I could never attain.

I needed to change the source of my joy and peace. With God's help, I realized that if I kept my joy and peace anchored in a secure, earthly future, I would never truly be joyful or at peace in my life, and I would be subject to the wind and waves of life and spend my life chasing a joy and peace that only God could give me. The true source of my anxiety and depression were being caused by my desire to capture an unattainable security and safety in this life. I discovered that my joy and peace are only truly secure in the confidence of my eternal relationship with God. I learned that whether life was going great or terrible, I could stay in joy and peace because my eternal future is secure in God. Changing my source of joy and peace allowed me to release the pressure I felt to worry and control all the uncontrollable variables in my life. I was able to begin to truly just rest in the knowledge that God was in control and that I could trust His plan for me.

In my anguish and torment of a major letdown, God was faithful. Today I can say that I am thankful that I had to travel through the desert, because if it wasn't for the struggle, I never would have had to turn to God. I never would have learned that the source of my joy and peace were the reason I had become shackled to anxiety, depression, and pain in the first place. I believe that sometimes, the only way we can grow and break free from the things that seek to enslave us is to go through the struggle. The great news for us is that we don't have to go through the struggle alone. He is with us, and He loves us.

Before we move on to the next chapter, I want to say that if you find yourself in a season of struggle or setback, just know that you are not alone and that you can make it through this challenging season. The Lord will never leave you or forsake you, and He is more than able to help you overcome this challenge. Just don't give up. If your struggle is overwhelming you, please don't feel ashamed to reach out for help. God places community in our lives so that we can support each other in the good times and bad. If you need help, please reach out to a trusted source for help. You will get through this!

> Dear heavenly Father, thank You for your ever-loving kindness and grace that You show us. Thank You, Lord, for allowing us to walk through challenging times so that we may grow and be set free from things that enslave us. Today, Lord, I come before You and ask for Your strength and courage for those who may be going through difficult and challenging times. I know that it is hard to see any good during difficult times, but, Lord, I ask that You give understanding to those who may be struggling today. Allow them to experience Your peace, and make Your ways known to them that they may overcome the challenge they are facing. Lord, thank You that You will never leave us or forsake us. Thank You for Your Holy Spirit who lives inside us, and thank You for saving us by the blood of Jesus Christ. In Jesus's name, amen!

Comforts of the Shackle

All the sons of Israel grumbled against Moses and Aaron; and
the whole congregation said to them, "Would that we had
died in the land of Egypt! Or would that we had died in this
wilderness! Why is the Lord bringing us into this land, to fall by
the sword? Our wives and our little ones will become plunder;
would it not be better for us to return to Egypt?" So they said
to one another, "Let us appoint a leader and return to Egypt."
—Numbers 14:2–4 (NASB)

In my journey of deliverance, I was set free from the crushing
anxiety, depression, and chronic pain that had completely turned my
life upside down. God had promised me through a miraculous sign
that my life would be made new. God was faithful when I experienced my first letdown and realized that my deliverance wasn't automatic. He gave me the courage and patience to trust His plan for my
deliverance. When I was struggling with lingering fears that tried to
keep me from moving forward, God was there to expose the root of
my fears. He gave me the boldness and confidence to take back the
life He had given me through His Holy Spirit. When I grew weary
and tired of the journey, He showed me that joy and peace don't
come from earthly circumstances, but that these things could only
be found in Him. Every step of the way, God was faithful to me. He
was faithful when my faith was high, and He was faithful even when
I was angry and blaming Him.

Looking back at everything I had gone through to this point, I
can now see how God was using my circumstances to prepare me for
the greatest challenge I went through in my journey of deliverance.

The greatest challenge I faced in this journey was withstanding the temptation to return to the false comfort of the shackle. I know it may sound a little crazy to think that someone would want to go back into slavery after being set free, but sadly, I believe this happens all too often. Have you ever seen someone who dramatically changed their life for the positive then witness them fall back into the lifestyle that they were delivered from? Have you ever wondered why someone would choose to go back?

Think about the last time you went to a great and challenging conference, retreat, or camp. Did it leave you feeling inspired and hungry to make some positive changes in your life? For me, while growing up, a common term used for this was "church camp high." Anytime I would leave church camp, I would leave fully inspired and on fire for the things of God. I immediately would put the lessons I learned to practice and began practically applying them in my life. Things would go great for a while, but then slowly but surely, the intense passion and fire I had for the lessons I learned would wane and, little by little, I would slip back into my same old routine that I was in before camp.

I often would question why my "camp highs" typically ended with life going back to normal. I've often wondered if these types of events are worth it if ultimately nothing in my life changed long term. I would wonder why these life-changing truths just didn't seem to stick in my life.

The truth of the matter is that the journey of deliverance is a difficult, challenging, and even painful walk that takes you out of your comfort zone. It often asks more from us than what we believe we can handle. It requires dedication, hard work, and, many times, toughness to overcome the pains of the journey. The journey often seems never ending, and it can be so exhausting spiritually, mentally, and physically. The pain and difficulty of the journey can make anything seem more desirable than continuing down the path to deliverance, and it often entices its travelers to stop for a rest. Jesus alluded to this struggle with the parable He told about the sower:

> And He spoke many things to them in parables,
> saying, "Behold, the sower went out to sow; and

as he sowed, some seeds fell beside the road, and the birds came and ate them up. Others fell on the rocky places, where they did not have much soil; and immediately they sprang up, because they had no depth of soil. But when the sun had risen, they were scorched; and because they had no root, they withered away. Others fell among the thorns, and the thorns came up and choked them out. And others fell on the good soil and yielded a crop, some a hundredfold, some sixty, and some thirty." (Matthew 13:3–8, NASB)

I believe what Jesus was saying here directly applies to a journey of deliverance. During the journey, life-changing lessons are learned and applied just like seed being sown on the ground. Then just like the birds, the shallow soil, the scorching sun, and the suffocating thorns, the distractions and difficulties of the struggle begin to slowly steal the seed and new growth from our lives. Eventually, the result for all the seed sown outside the good soil is harvest that never comes to fruition. This example is much like a life that began to transform and had the potential to change but ultimately didn't. This was me all my life growing up, and it almost was me again in my journey.

For me, the temptation to seek comfort in the shackle came in the form of growing weary of battling the physical pain, the anxiety, and the ever-revolving bouts with depression. It seemed as if I was constantly fighting a battle from the moment I woke up to the moment I laid down. Sometimes the physical pain hurt so much and was so constant that all I could do was cry. The anxiety would often try to overtake me and sweep me away like raging waters to a ship in the sea. Then, when I would have days that were setbacks, the depression would come on strong, and it would overshadow everything in my life. Choosing to stand up and fight was tiring, and I began to be tempted to give up. I knew if I gave up, I would be miserably unhappy, but at least I wouldn't have to fight anymore. I was tempted by the thoughts that told me that giving up would be okay because at least I wouldn't have to be constantly taking on challenges that were just too much for me to handle alone.

Deliverance will almost always require you to step out of your comfort zone and challenge yourself in ways that you typically wouldn't challenge yourself on your own. This is what makes the return to slavery so enticing. When I decided to trust God and begin my journey of deliverance from anxiety, depression, and chronic pain, I started to make courageous choices that would challenge the anxiety, the depression, and the pain. Daily life became a battle to overcome the things that once held me captive. The victories that I was experiencing were often encouraging, and they kept me motivated to keep pushing. But as days passed and the battles didn't seem to get any easier, I started to become discouraged and exhausted. I couldn't help but think, *Why I am working so hard to overcome something that doesn't seem to get any better?* Maybe I just needed to accept the fact that anxiety, depression, and chronic pain were just going to be a normal part of my life. And there it was—the temptation to return to the false comfort of the shackle. I was at a fork in the road of my journey. Would I return to my Egypt and allow my harvest to be stolen, or would I press forward? I needed to decide. I knew the right thing to do was to keep pressing forward, but I was just so tired. Finally, I wrote this poem to the Lord to air out the temptation and struggle I was going through:

My past calls unto me as on old friend.
It reminds me of feelings of happiness and good times.
It beckons me to drink of its sweet cup.
It calls me to rest and kick back.
But beware of those who drink of its cup.
The devoted think to themselves,
"One sip of refreshment and one moment to sit back
will help ease my journey
and bring refreshment to my weary soul."
Little do they know that the enemy waits behind a wall
with ropes ready to bind their very souls.
The desire is as strong as an itch to be scratched,

> it's as natural as taking a breath.
> Who then can overcome such temptation?
> What hope is there for the devoted?
> But I cry out to my Lord and Savior.
> He is more than a conqueror.
> He is strong in my weakness.
> He is more than able to overcome.
> I turn my eyes from myself and look to the heavens.
> My strength is renewed, and my joy is restored.
> In Him I find my rest.

All the distractions and challenges of the journey had taken their toll on me. I felt like I was teetering on returning to my old dead life that was shackled to the anxiety, depression, and chronic pain. It was about to be the same old "church camp high" story for me until the Lord showed me that through Him, I was more than able to continue my journey. Even when I didn't have the strength or motivation to continue, His Holy Spirit would be there to help me continue the journey. God had prepared me for this moment. He had strengthened me and helped me grow to this point in my journey. While the temptation to return seemed big, God's word and the testimony of His love and faithfulness in my journey overshadowed them and made them seem small. He had helped my faith in Him grow strong, and He built spiritual fortitude in me that helped me make the choice to continue my journey. I decided to forsake the shackle and to continue to press forward. I didn't know if the journey would be ending soon, or if it would last a lifetime, but one thing I did know was that God's grace was sufficient for me and that He would be faithful through the rest of my journey.

Making this decision was big for me because it completely changed the trajectory of my life. When I made this choice, I started seeing this journey as something I could embrace, and not something that just needed to be endured. I began to embrace the struggle of the journey because I realized that I could hear and receive from the Lord in a way that was unique to someone going through extreme struggles. I began to see the journey as an opportunity to build my fortitude, and I began to appreciate the journey because it opened my eyes to the fact that there is a world full of people who feel hopeless and trapped in their own battles with anxiety, depression, or pain. I didn't always get it perfectly, and I had my weak moments that sometimes caused me to take steps backward, but God was right there to pick me up and encourage me to keep pushing forward.

Sadly, in the Exodus account, the people of Israel gave into the fear of the challenges they would need to overcome to complete their journey. The shackles of their slavery in Egypt seemed so much better than the uncertainty and challenges they faced ahead. Despite the faithfulness of God through their entire journey, they still didn't trust Him to help them enter into their deliverance. Unfortunately for them, this surrender to fear ended up costing an entire generation the ability to enter the promised land that God had for them and caused the entire nation to wander in the desert for forty years. (See Numbers 14.)

The sobering reality of this account is that we often face decisions in our lives that put our faith to the test and can cause unnecessary wandering in our own personal deserts when we chose our ways over His ways. Jeremiah 29:11 tells us that the Lord has "plans for welfare and not for calamity to give you a future and a hope." God has wonderful plans for each of our lives. Yes, He even has a good plan for those of us going through something as terrible as anxiety, depression, and chronic pain. The big question we all must answer in our individual journeys is this: "Do I chose the shackle, or will I trust the Lord and keep moving forward?"

Before we continue to our last chapter together, I want to encourage you if you are struggling with the decision to quit your journey. I know this journey is not easy, and it often feels like you are all alone. Sometimes the torment and anguish of the journey can seem overwhelming, and it feels like you just can't go any further. If you're desperate for a sign or a word from the Lord because you are at the end of the rope, here it is. Though I am in the middle of writing this book right now, I believe there is someone out there that needs to know that the Lord sees you. He knows you. He knows the pain you are going through, and He is right there beside you. Don't give up, press into Him, and ask Him for help. God can overwhelm the things that seek to overwhelm you. I'm rooting for you, and I know you can make the decision to continue your journey toward deliverance. You can do this! Let's pray.

> Dear heavenly Father, thank You for the journey that we are on right now. Thank You for Your faithfulness through this difficult and tiresome journey. Right now, Father, I come before You and ask You to give this reader the fortitude necessary to make the choice to continue their fight. Lord, rejuvenate their tired and fatigued spirits, minds, and bodies. Give them Your peace as they press forward and open their hearts, minds, and spirits to receive all that You have for them in this journey. I ask that You bless every one of these readers and allow them to know You in a way they never have known You before. Thank You again for never leaving us or forsaking us. We love You, Lord! In Jesus's name, amen!

Courage to Inherit
the Promise

Have I not commanded you? Be strong and
courageous! Do not tremble or be dismayed, for the
Lord your God is with you wherever you go.
                                         —Joshua 1:9 (NASB)

When anxiety, depression, and pain took over my life back in the fall of 2016, I thought my life was over. I was scared, angry, and bitter because I thought it wasn't fair that I had to go through something as terrible as what I was dealing with. I would look around at all my family, friends, and strangers, and I would be so envious of them getting to live a normal life. I remember thinking how lucky they were to have a life that seemed to be free from worry, free from the dark stormy clouds of depression, and free of physical pain. I felt so sorry for myself. I was a terrible person to be around, and I was quickly destroying all my relational bridges because I had just shut down. I no longer knew how to have fun, relax, joke around, or just be an enjoyable person to be around. I was completely and utterly shackled to anxiety, depression, and pain. My life lost all meaning outside of my extreme worries, my sadness, and the excruciating pain I would deal with daily.

Then when all hope seemed lost and I seemed doomed to end my days in misery, God stepped in to deliver me. It seems like every step of the way, I always seemed to think that God was going to just take my anxiety, depression, and pain in a moment. I secretly hoped that the next victory would be the victory that would suddenly drop my struggles like a boxer who just got KO'd. What I didn't know at the time was that God was doing a greater work in me that was at a much higher level than I could have imagined.

> "For My thoughts are not your thoughts, nor are your ways My ways," declares the Lord. "For as the heavens are higher than the earth, so are My ways higher than your ways and My thoughts than your thoughts. (Isaiah 55:8–9, NASB)

When I cried out to God to help me and deliver me, I thought simply being delivered was enough. I thought that getting relief from the things that were tormenting me would be enough, but God had so much more for me that I didn't even realize that I needed.

> Now to Him who is able to do far more abundantly beyond all that we ask or think, according to the power that works within us. (Ephesians 3:20, NASB)

While I was thinking immediate short-term deliverance, God was preparing me for a life-changing deliverance that would set me free from the things that had enslaved me. God used my journey to cause a rebirth of my relationship with Him. God used my journey to build my faith and my fortitude, and He gave me a testimony to help encourage others who find themselves struggling to be delivered from their captor.

When I first started this journey, I hated everything about my circumstances, but as I look back on the journey and all that I went through with God by my side, I can't help but be grateful for the journey. I truly believe that this journey saved both my physical and spiritual life. I am so overwhelmed at just how much God loves me. It makes me tear up when I think about the fact that He loves me so much that He was willing to walk me through my journey because it would save me. God wanted to save me, and I firmly believe that today, He wants to save you!

After wandering forty years in the desert, Israel finally was ready to cross over into the promised land. Israel's journey to deliverance was marked with many miracles and mistakes, but the Lord was faithful to bring them to His promised land. Led by Joshua, the people of Israel did cross the Jordan river and began the task of possessing the land that the Lord had promised to His chosen people. You can read all about how they did this in the book of Joshua.

> Pass through the midst of the camp and command the people, saying, "Prepare provisions for yourselves, for within three days you are to cross this Jordan, to go in to possess the land which the Lord your God is giving you to possess it."
> (Joshua 1:11, NASB)

One important detail that I would like to point out about Israel's promised land was that there were still inhabitants and obstacles in the land that they had to overcome to take possession of it. Possessing their promise wasn't simply crossing a river and settling on an uninhabited land. Possessing the land meant taking on challenges that were far too great for them to overcome on their own. Possessing the promise was going to require their reliance on God.

Today, for you and me, the promised land can mean so many things. Eternally the promised land is a symbol of rest in the Lord and living with Him for all eternity. Earthside, the promised land can be a symbol of the victory you need over a specific challenge in your life. For me, the promised land was victory over anxiety, depression, and chronic pain. It meant entering God's rest and peace. It meant a rebirth of my life. It also meant more battles and challenges that I could only overcome with the help of God. Entering the promised land, just as in the case with Israel, isn't automatic. In my journey I have found that entering the promises of God almost always meant fighting an enemy that only God could overcome, but if we choose to trust in Him and allow Him to lead, we can inherit His promise of deliverance.

So what does this practically look like in my journey? For me, entering the promised land meant taking on the anxiety, depression, and pain and no longer allowing them to dictate my life. Victory, in my case, wasn't an absence of the symptoms of anxiety, depression, and pain. My victory came in the form of peace, boldness, and confidence despite dealing with symptoms of anxiety, depression, and pain. These former tormentors no longer have the power to control me or determine the joy and peace in my life. While I will continue to ask the Lord for healing from the symptoms of these challenges, I can joyfully and peacefully rest in the reality of God's freedom.

Today I want to ask you a question: are you ready to take that step of courage and faith to inherit the promise of rest that God wants to give you? I know it's scary, difficult, and overwhelming to try to break free from something that you feel is inescapable, but I want you to know that you are more than a conqueror through Jesus Christ. (See Romans 8:37.) God loves you, and He can help you gain victory over the shackles that have enslaved you. Please take encouragement from my story. If God can deliver someone like me, an average guy with nothing superspecial about him, and deliver me from life-crushing enslavement to complete victory, then He can most certain do it for you too! I know I just said it, but it's worth repeating. If God can deliver someone like me, an average guy with nothing superspecial about him, and deliver me from life-crushing enslavement to complete victory, then He can most certain do it for you too! He loves you, and He wants to help. Don't let another day pass where you suffer under the cruel shackle of your captor. Today take a step of faith toward deliverance. Be bold in the Lord and dare yourself to dream of a life free from the shackle. A life of freedom is possible for you. It's time to leave your Egypt.

Peace be with you!

> Be strong and courageous, do not be afraid or tremble at them, for the Lord your God is the one who goes with you. He will not leave you or forsake you. (Deuteronomy 31:6, NASB)

Father God, I thank You for the opportunity to help minister to those who are hurting and feeling hopeless. Father, I thank You for the reader who is reading this book today. I ask You, Lord, to bless them and speak to them. Lord, You know the challenges this reader is facing, and You know the journey they have ahead of them. I ask that You help them to know Your unending love and faithfulness. Lord, I ask You to bless them with the courage to go on the journey of their deliverance. Let Your words be a light to their feet and a lamp for their path. Keep them in Your ways and deliver them into Your rest. Thank You, Lord, for Your grace, Your love, and Your mercy. In Jesus's name, amen.

About the Author

Isaac Nathaniel Gonzalez was driven to become an author by his passion to help others struggling with anxiety, depression, and chronic pain. He has a master's degree in business administration and loves working on process improvement. Isaac is madly in love with his wife, Brandi, and loves doing life with her, their three kids, and their Yorkie.